MW01377713

BIBLE DOG STORIES
WHERE DOGS ALWAYS LOOK GOOD
AND CATS ALWAYS LOOK BAD
Written and Illustrated
By Cynthia Lovell

First Edition

NEWMAN SPRINGS PUBLISHING
320 Broad Street
Red Bank, NJ 07701

First originally published by Newman Springs Publishing 2023

ISBN 979-8-88763-253-7 (Paperback)
ISBN 979-8-88763-255-1 (Hardcover)
ISBN 979-8-88763-254-4 (Digital)

Printed in the United States of America

To my children,
their children and grandchildren
and the furry angels who inspired the
writing of this book.

Contents

Introduction

Bible Dog is the storyteller in this book and represents all dogs who were around to see, hear, and pass down stories about life in Bible days. Bible Dog noticed that humans sometimes missed very important details, such as the bad behavior of cats. Sometimes cats were just observers. But at other times, cats caused trouble. Bible Dog's job in some of these stories is to point out that dogs are good and let the reader draw conclusions about cats.

Bible Dog stated, "I have a few cat friends. I do not understand their ways. But they are my friends, and I love them. I guess the whole point of these stories (if you don't focus on how annoying cats can be) is that God wants us to be kind to each other and to share and know that God's love includes people and animals who don't always act nice or look like us."

THE REAL STORY OF ADAM AND EVE INCLUDES A CAT

GENESIS 1

Adam and Eve lived in a beautiful garden called Eden. The garden had all kinds of plants, trees, and animals. God told them to have fun and enjoy the garden. God warned them to stay away from one bad tree in the garden. They said, "Okay," and went off to play.

A sneaky cat laid his ears back and pretended to be a snake. He crawled along the ground hissing and showing his sharp fangs. He told Adam and Eve they should definitely try some of the apples on that tree. Bible Dog, of course, tried to stop them.

Adam and Eve started a big fight to see who could get to that tree first. But the cat tripped Adam.

Adam fell flat on his face. Eve got the first bite of that apple. And that cat laughed!

This is when dogs first learned that cats are sneaky and that humans sometimes make bad choices and pick bad apples.

HOW CATS BARELY MADE IT THROUGH THE FLOOD

GENESIS 6

As everyone knows, cats are very stubborn. They also have bad attitudes. This story proves it. In the early Bible days, God told a man named Noah that a big flood was coming. He also told Noah to build an ark big enough to hold two of every kind of animal. Noah worked and worked. He finally finished building the ark. Bible Dog helped Noah. The cat did not help at all.

When the rain started, Noah called for all the animals to get into the ark.

Of course, dogs came as they were told. So did all the other animals, except for you-know-who. Yep! Cats just pretended they did not hear Noah. They kept fighting, grooming, and ignoring.

Down, down, down came the rain. And *up, up, up* came the flood. The ark started floating away. The animals inside were safe and warm. Pretty soon there was no dry ground. Those cats had to swim to the ark. They were swimming and yelling and crying.

Noah had to throw a little boat out to those cats and tie it to the ark. That was how cats barely made it through the flood. For their own safety, they should have paid attention and done as they were told. Thank goodness they didn't get to ride in the ark with the rest of us nice animals.

HANNAH NANNY BOO BOO

1 SAMUEL 1

Poor Hannah. First she had to share her husband, Elky, with a very mean lady named Penny. Penny had many children. Hannah didn't have any children. The worst part was that Penny laughed and played mean tricks on Hannah. She thought she was much better than Hannah because she had kids, and Hannah didn't.

Every year Hannah asked God for a baby. And every year God must have gotten mixed up and gave that mean Penny another baby instead of Hannah. It got so bad that when Hannah prayed, old Penny lined up all her kids and teased Hannah. Hannah cried and cried and kept on praying.

Hannah's husband thought he was helping by telling Hannah nice things like, "Hey! You have me! Aren't I worth more than a hundred sons!" And he gave Hannah extra presents. He just didn't understand at all. Hannah just sighed and made a promise to God that if God would give her a baby son, she would give him right back to God at the temple.

The next time Hannah went to the temple, an old priest named Eli saw Hannah praying and praying. He thought she was either crazy or drunk because her lips were moving, but no sounds were coming out.

When she told Eli about all she had been through because of that mean Penny, that priest told her that her prayers would be answered.

Hannah was so happy that she skipped all the way home. "Hey! Cheer down!" yelled Penny.

Hannah began rocking and knitting. She had a big smile on her face.

Penny did not like what she was seeing one little bit. But Hannah did not care.

Hannah's prayers were answered. She finally had a little baby son and named him Samuel. When he was old enough, she took him to the temple to meet old Priest Eli.

This story shows that dogs are loyal and kind. And even though Penny, her kids, and even her cat acted mean to Hannah, Hannah never gave up. She kept praying. She kept her promise. And she never smacked Penny!

DANIEL AND THE WONDER BOYS VERSUS THE CATS IN CHARGE

DANIEL 1-3

King Neb of Babylon captured Daniel and his friends Shadrach, Meshach, and Abednego from their homes in Judah. King Neb immediately noticed that Daniel and his friends were strong, smart, and handsome. The king also noticed that these young men did not eat candy or drink sugary drinks. They ate vegetables and lean meat, even though King Neb offered them all kinds of junk food like donuts and cookies.

After some time, the king also noticed how wise and healthy Daniel and his friends were. So he called them the Wonder Boys.

The king also had a large pack of cats who served as leaders and guards.

These cats worshipped their king. They also worshipped tree stumps.

Daniel and his friends were wise because they read their Bible and made time every day to be quiet and listen to God.

The king realized that Daniel and the Wonder Boys knew more and acted nicer than his cat leaders and guards.

It wasn't long before King Neb told his cat leaders he wouldn't be needing them anymore because Daniel and the Wonder Boys were better.

The king began to depend on Daniel for advice. He even asked Daniel to interpret his weird dreams.

The cats knew right then they had to get rid of Daniel and the Wonder Boys. They formed a little band and called it the Racket Katz Band. Then they convinced the king to make a rule that everyone had to throw themselves on the ground and worship a statue of the king whenever the Racket Katz played their music.

King Neb loved the band's idea and made his royal loudspeaker drive around to announce his new rule.

Of course, the first place the Racket Katz played their horrible music was in Daniel's room. Daniel thought worshipping people and tree stumps was ridiculous. So he asked the cats to leave and kept on working.

That's all those cats were waiting for. They made a beeline straight to the king to tattletale about Daniel breaking the rule.

The king called the Wonder Boys to see if they would bow down to his statue or if they would also break his new rule. But they refused to bow down and worship anyone but God.

The king was furious. He had his guard throw Shadrach, Meshach, and Abednego into the fiery furnace. He even had his guard make the fire extra hot.

The king was amazed when he looked into that furnace and saw what looked like an angel walking around with Shadrach, Meshach, and Abednego. They were all cool and calm. He called for them to get out of that furnace.

Then King Neb put Shadrach, Meshach, and Abednego up on a stage and announced to everyone in his kingdom that the God of Daniel and the Wonder Boys was good and strong.

He also said that anyone who disrespected Daniel or the Wonder Boys or their God would be thrown into an electric mixer and mashed up.

JONAH HATES HIS ASSIGNMENT

JONAH 3 AND 4

The people of Nineveh had been terrible bullies to the people of Israel. Jonah was from Israel and hated the people of Nineveh. Mainly he was scared of them. But God wanted Jonah to go to Nineveh and tell those people how much God loved them.

Even though Jonah said, "Okay. Sure," to God, he took off his sandals and put on his running shoes. Bible Dog wondered what Jonah was planning.

Maybe God won't notice, Jonah thought as he ran toward the sea and away from Nineveh.

Once he was on the boat, Jonah fell asleep. When a bad storm came, the sailors thought God sent the storm because Jonah was bad luck.

They prayed and rolled dice just to be sure they were doing the right thing. Then they threw Jonah overboard. Jonah, who was still sleeping, was surprised when he woke up in the sea.

Poor Jonah. He gulped so much water that he sank to the bottom of the sea.

Then he saw a huge whale swimming toward him. Jonah thought he was going to die. But that whale was sent from God and swallowed Jonah right up.

It was dark and scary and smelly inside that whale. Jonah began to think and pray. He decided to try what God told him to do.

You would have thought God would have been sick of Jonah by now, but it was the whale who really got sick of Jonah.

The whale yakked Jonah up onto the beach.

As soon as Jonah was yakked up onto that beach, he marched right to Nineveh and set up a big tent in which to preach about God's love.

There were some local cats in Nineveh who were bored and curious. So they climbed to the top of the tent and started tearing it up. They began to cut the wires holding up the tent. When the dogs saw what the cats were doing, they went crazy. One dog barked and barked. The other dog tried to get to the cats by sawing down the poles the cats were standing on.

The dogs did not realize the poles were also holding up the tent. So the tent fell on top of Jonah and all the people! Jonah left the crumpled tent and Nineveh and walked into the desert. He had secretly been hoping God would be mad at the people of Nineveh and do some spectacular awfulness to them. Instead, God loved them! And they changed their ways after listening to Jonah's message.

Jonah sat in the hot sun and pouted. God felt sorry for him and made a big vine grow up and provide shade for him. But Jonah still pouted, and we will never know why.

Even though the cats almost ruined everything, the people of Nineveh listened to Jonah and began to act nicer. The dogs learned not to go crazy when they see cats. The cats unfortunately learned nothing about taking responsibility for their actions.

WHERE THAT WEDDING WINE REALLY WENT
YES, CATS WERE INVOLVED
JOHN 2:1-11

Jesus, His family, and all the people in His town were very excited. Two young people were getting married, and everyone was invited to the party. Jesus's mom was helping with the party. The cats were watching and already causing trouble.

On the day of the wedding, everyone was laughing and dancing and eating and drinking and having a good time. The cats were nowhere to be found. Bible Dog did not miss them at all.

Jesus's mom came up to Him. She had a worried look on her face and began talking to Him.

Then Jesus's mom called the maid and told her to do whatever Jesus said.

Jesus followed the maid into the kitchen. They could not believe their eyes. There were seven cats all laid out on the floor and everywhere. Their tongues were hanging out, and their eyes were rolled back. And their bellies were about to pop. They had drunk all the wine their selfish selves. They didn't even care about that poor mama and daddy or the bride and groom.

Jesus just shook His head and performed that nice miracle of changing water into the most delicious wine anyone had ever drunk.

This story shows that no matter how much those selfish cats tried, they couldn't spoil everyone's good time with Jesus around.

JESUS, DEMONS, PIGS, AND CATS!

LUKE 8:26–39

In this story, Bible Dog shows that cats are awful, and dogs are kind and useful. In a place called Gerasene, the farmers were having a terrible time with their herds and flocks. Something was scaring their cows and little children. Some people blamed it on the noisy pigs. But other people blamed it on a homeless man named Ernest, who barely wore any clothes and said he had demons.

Another possibility is that cats were to blame for the terrible times the farmers, kids, and other animals were having.

HEY! I GOT DEMONS!
BANG! BANG!
BOOM! BOOM!
YIKES!

Jesus and His disciples had just arrived in Gerasene when they heard Ernest yelling. Ernest had dirty, tangled hair, a dirty face, and brown teeth. He smelled bad and spit when he yelled.

Everybody screamed and ran away except Jesus, the loyal dog, and a nearby herd of terrible cats. The disciples were scared, so they hid behind some trees at the bottom of the hill.

When Jesus asked Ernest to come down and talk, Ernest screamed and jumped out of the tree into the herd of cats.

As usual, the cats overreacted and jumped off a cliff.

Jesus told Ernest those demons left him and went with those cats that jumped off the cliff.

Ernest then combed his hair, washed his face, brushed his teeth, and put on clean clothes. He sat with Jesus and asked if he could come with Jesus. Jesus told Ernest that his family needed to see him and hear his good news. So Ernest said goodbye and left.

Many people think it was a herd of pigs that Jesus made those demons jump into when He threw them out of Ernest.

But it could have been a herd of cats who looked and sounded like pigs, as they often do. Those cats could've dressed up like pigs to get the pigs in trouble. Cats can be sneaky and scary. It could have been those cats that made Ernest have demons jump into him in the first place. The most important thing was that Jesus helped Ernest. It doesn't really matter whether those demons left with the pigs or cats. The demons finally left Ernest alone, thanks to Jesus.

WAYNE SHARES HIS LUNCH
BETTER WATCH THAT CAT!

JOHN 6:1-13 AND MATTHEW 14:13-21

Jesus and His disciples were out in the desert. A large crowd of people followed them to be near Jesus and hear Him talk. The disciples were getting tired and hungry. They told Jesus to send the people home to get food and rest. Jesus had another idea.

The disciples tried to find food. They were about to give up when a little boy named Wayne said he would share his fish and bread with everyone. The disciples took Wayne right to Jesus. Jesus smiled at Wayne and thanked him for offering his food.

Everyone had their eyes closed while Jesus said grace. That was when a sneaky cat crawled to the fish basket and ate as many fish as he could. When the prayer was over, everyone heard that cat burp. Bible Dog worried that the food was all gone. But Jesus made sure everyone had as much as they wanted. There was even food left over. So even if the cat didn't ruin the day, he sure tried.

Here's what I was hoping Jesus would say.

JESUS AND THE ROCK THROWERS

JOHN 8:1-11

This story is not really about cats. Even cats could not believe what happened one day after a big religious rally. There were some preachers and important men at that rally who spied and peeked in people's windows to see if anyone was breaking any rules.

These men caught a woman named Edna Jean with a man who was sneaking away from his wife. They brought her to Jesus and said, "Hey! Our rules say we should throw rocks at this woman. What do you say?" Jesus said, "Sure. Go ahead. But let the person who hasn't ever done anything bad or made a mistake throw the first rock."

ON THE COUNT OF THREE
ONE
TWO
THREE
WAIT!

It got really quiet. Jesus began writing and drawing in the dirt. One by one, starting with the leader, those men dropped their rocks and began sneaking away. Some of those guys even gave Jesus mean looks. But Jesus wasn't looking at them. He was paying attention to His writing and to Edna Jean.

WELL, EDNA JEAN. YOUR ROCK THROWERS ARE GONE. AND I'M SURE NOT GOING TO THROW ROCKS AT YOU. YOU SHOULD ALWAYS KNOW YOU ARE LOVED AND IMPORTANT.

FISHING WITH JESUS

CATS ARE NO HELP AT ALL

JOHN 21:2–12

The disciples were so sleepy. They had been fishing all night. It was now early in the morning, and their nets were still empty.

They saw someone waving to them from the beach. It was Jesus. He felt sorry for them and yelled for them to cast their net on the other side of the boat. They had already cast their net on both sides of their boat with no luck. But they did what He said just to be polite.

They threw their net to the other side of their boat. Sure enough, hundreds of fish jumped into those nets. While the disciples were smiling, cheering, and waving at Jesus, a group of cats jumped into their net. They made themselves at home and began eating the fish. Bible Dog was watching everything from the beach and tried to let the guys know what the cats were doing and why the nets were so heavy. But the disciples were busy trying to lift the heavy net into the boat and did not notice the cats.

Bible Dog was very worried that those cats would eat all the fish and leave none for Jesus and the disciples. Thankfully there were plenty of fish left. Jesus cooked the fish, and there was enough for everyone.

Once again, the cats tried to ruin everything. But, once again, Jesus stayed calm and fed everyone—even those selfish cats!

URF!
HEY JESUS! LOOK AT US!
YAY! WE GOT FISH!
MINNOW

NOT-SO-NICE DISCIPLE STORY NO. 1

JESUS, LITTLE KIDS, AND GRUMPY DISCIPLES

MARK 10:13–16

Bible Dog noticed some not-so-nice things about the disciples. They were sometimes very mean and selfish. For example, when a very nice little girl and a boy ran up to Jesus and jumped on Him, a disciple tried to chase them away. Jesus, who loves little kids, knew how to get His disciple to behave.

NOT-SO-NICE DISCIPLE STORY NO. 2
WHO'S THE GREATEST?
MARK 10:35–44

Right after Jesus scolded that disciple for yelling at the little kids, the disciples started arguing with each other about which one was Jesus's favorite. They had a big fight. They spit, shoved, pinched, yelled, and even wrestled. They were going around and around. They made so much noise that even the cats stopped their selfishness to watch!

HE LIKES ME BEST, YOU DONKEY!
I'M GREATEST, YOU PEA-BRAINED SQUIRREL-HEAD!
OW! MY FOOT!
Y'ALL ARE ALL GOING TO BE SORRY!!
GRRR

NOT-SO-NICE DISCIPLE STORY NO. 3
HEY! SHE'S NOT ONE OF US!

MARK 7:24-30

Once a woman from a different country came to Jesus. She asked Him to cast a demon out of her little girl. At first, Jesus did not say a word. Maybe He wanted to teach His disciples something. Then He pretended He agreed with what they were saying.

HAH! THAT'S TELLING HER, JESUS!
I SHOULD NOT GIVE GOOD FOOD THAT BELONGS TO THESE CHILDREN TO DOGS.

BUT YOUR HONOR.
EVEN THE DOGS
GET CRUMBS THE
CHILDREN DROP
ON THE FLOOR,
WOW!
OH YEAH!

Jesus and the disciples were amazed at how much faith that woman had. She never gave up or got touchy when Jesus teased her. She believed Jesus would make her little girl well, even if she was from a different country and a different church.

JESUS WALKS ON WATER
OH! NO! THE CATS AGAIN!

JOHN 6:1-16

The disciples and other people who followed Jesus wanted to make Jesus their hero and take over the government. The disciples led cheers and chants. Jesus could not believe what He saw. He told the disciples to pipe down and get in their boat. He said He needed quiet time and would meet them across the lake.

JESUS! JESUS! HE'S OUR MAN!
JESUS FOR KING!
YEAH! KICK CAESAR OUT!

THESE PEOPLE JUST WEAR HIM OUT!
SNORE.

It was nighttime by the time the disciples got their boat out to sea. The boat started shaking and rolling. They thought they were in a bad storm and about to drown. What they did not see was a herd of mean cats who had paddled through the water just to scare the disciples. Those cats rocked the boat back and forth and splashed water on them.

Jesus saw what was happening from where He was praying and resting. He came down to make His disciples calm down once again. He walked right across the water. They thought they were seeing a ghost and got even more scared. Jesus yelled out to them so they would know it was Him and not a ghost. The cats just watched. They thought it was funny to see those disciples being scared.

Peter was so excited, he stepped right onto the water.

OH NO! THE CATS AGAIN! HELP!!

Peter was walking on water just fine until those cats showed up again. They splashed water on him and scared him. He began yelling for help.

The cats tried to ruin the good things Jesus did, but once again, the good things Jesus did could not be ruined. And once again, even if the disciples acted silly, scared, or mean, Jesus never quit loving them and hanging out with them.

And there you have it. Cats with their sneaky selfishness, dogs with their wonderful goodness, and humans—even those disciples—with their fear and misunderstanding could never ruin God's love for everyone or the good things Jesus did.

Acknowledgments

I am grateful for a long history of love, laughter, and humor with my daughters, Jamie Suel and Jodi Price. I am also grateful to my father, who introduced me to the drawing of cartoons, and to my mother for her first response to these stories many years ago. She laughed out loud but was concerned about irreverence. I like to think she finds the stories even funnier now that she is in heaven where she can relax about reverence. Thanks to Anne Mugler for the encouragement over many years of friendship that propelled this work into published form. I am grateful for love and encouragement from my daughters and their families. Thank you to my human angel, Doris Miller, and my spirit angel, Robin Webb, for generous, loving support.

About the Author

Cynthia Lovell, humorist, storyteller, and artist, earned her master of science degree in education and counseling at the University of North Texas. She began writing and illustrating humorous stories when her daughters were small. As they grew up and went to college, she sent them little cat and dog tales, along with Bible story cartoons. She enjoys working in clay, cartooning, and card-making. She also creates folk art from discarded stuff. Her unpublished works include *Minreeka Perkle's Life in Twicks and Beyond; How to Train Your Dog to Be More Like a Cat; The Wonderfulness of Cats—A Fairy Tale that Explains It All;* and *What Makes Dogs Better Than Cats—Letter to a Young Dog.*

Printed in the USA
CPSIA information can be obtained
at www.ICGtesting.com
LVHW070306030823
753916LV00002B/15